*E*ASY TO MAKE
CROSS STITCH
KEEPSAKES

EASY TO MAKE
CROSS STITCH
KEEPSAKES
STELLA EDWARDS

BROCKHAMPTON PRESS
LONDON

First published in Great Britain in 1994
by Anaya Publishers Ltd, Strode House,
44-50 Osnaburgh Street, London NW1 3ND

This edition published 1996 by Brockhampton Press,
a member of Hodder Headline PLC Group

Editor Helen Douglas-Cooper
Design Millions Design
Photography Steve Tanner
Charts Anthony Duke
Illustrators Kate Simunek, Terry Evans

British Library Cataloguing in Publication Data

Edwards, Stella
Easy to Make Cross Stitch Keepsakes
I. Title
746.44

ISBN 1-86019-174-6

Typeset by Servis Filmsetting Ltd, Manchester, UK
Colour reproduction by Scantrans Pte Ltd, Singapore
Printed and bound in EC

CONTENTS

Introduction

Cross stitch is a popular and simple form of embroidery that provides a wonderful way to create reminders of important events or treasured memories for someone special.

According to the dictionary 'keepsake' has been defined as 'anything which serves as a reminder of a person or event' and in this book I have tried to do just that; creating designs which you can make to give to a special friend or close relation, which are personal to them and will remind them of you each time they look at the gift. I have also tried to make the designs adaptable. For example, initials can be added to a lot of the patterns to make them individual, colours can be changed as a reminder of the person's favourite flowers or their favourite colour, and designs can be made larger or smaller by changing the fabric they are embroidered on.

The selection of embroidery fabrics available is tremendous and by experimentation you will discover the fabric that you find the easiest to work with and which gives you the most pleasure. In this book I have used embroidery fabric ranging from 11 holes per inch (2.5cm) up to 22 holes per inch but each design can be stitched on a different fabric to that recommended here. To make larger Christmas decorations, for example, embroider the designs on 14- or 11-count fabric rather than the 18-count, or make the Elephant diary design into a bell-pull by stitching it on a 14-count fabric instead of 18 and stitch more elephants!

As well as the vast range of fabrics there is a lot of merchandise available specially created for cross-stitch embroiderers. These include such items as card mounts, which come in a range of sizes, shapes, colours and textured finishes. Special cards for Christmas, congratulations and birthdays can be found as well as plain cards. By looking around and seeing the variety on offer, you can choose the mount that most suits your design and the person you are giving it to, which will make it most distinctive.

Apart from card mounts there is also a variety of picture mounts available. Round, square, oblong and rectangular are easily found in a great selection of shapes and colours. There are also special mounts for Christmas decorations in the shapes of bells, trees, diamonds, hearts and so on; all of which gives you great scope in making your design special.

Cross stitch is a very easy stitch to learn, and once mastered all manner of designs can be created. In this book I have kept to the basic cross stitch, but used a three-quarter cross stitch and quarter cross stitch to get a smooth line around a design where, in cases, a softer curve is required. I have also used french knots in a couple of designs, which add interest to the design and create a textured finish. I have also used the four-sided square stitch, which is perfect as a border edge where you want a frayed fringe. This is demonstrated in the two herbal sachets. And, of course, there is a back stitch, which is so simple and so effective as an outline to a design or to define a particular area within the embroidery.

Once you have learnt how to do the basic cross stitch and embroidered your first design, you will find you will want to do more and more! I hope that through this book you will be inspired to adapt some of my designs to your own needs and create something really distinctive that will truly become a 'keepsake' and be treasured for always.

Note: Anchor thread numbers are given in the text. A conversion chart on page 80 gives the equivalent DMC thread numbers.

Fruit and Flowers

Poppies card

A lovely card for a friend's summer birthday or to send as a special thank-you message. The design can be mounted in a red, yellow, white or green card.

Materials
1 piece Aida cream fabric 18 holes per inch (2.5cm) size 4½ × 3½in (11.25 × 8.75cm)
Anchor stranded cotton: one skein each of 239 olive green (dark), 267 lime green (light), 290 yellow, 323 peach, 335 red, 403 black
Card mount

Preparation
1 Measure and mark the middle of the fabric with vertical and horizontal rows of basting stitches (refer to Better Techniques).

Working the embroidery
2 The centre of the chart is indicated by arrows on each side. This coincides with the basting stitches. Following the chart and colour key, begin by embroidering the middle block of colour using 2 strands of thread together. Complete the design as shown on the chart.

Finishing
3 Remove the basting stitches. Press the finished embroidery lightly on the wrong side.

4 Trim the edges of the fabric to fit the card, leaving as much allowance as possible around the actual embroidery (refer to Better Techniques).

5 Spread glue thinly around the edges of the window on the inside of the card. Position the embroidery behind the window, and stick it down.

6 Spread glue round the edges of the left-hand panel and fold it over the embroidery. Press down firmly and leave to dry thoroughly.

Size of finished embroidery:
2½ × 1½in (6.25 × 3.75cm)

KEY

■ 239
□ 267
▨ 290
▨ 323
▨ 335
■ 403

11

Water-lily picture

This picture is a wonderful reminder of lazy summer days picnicking by lakes and ponds, watching the dragonflies dive and swoop among the water-lilies.

Materials
1 piece of Aida white fabric 14 holes per inch (2.5cm) size 7 × 9in (17.5 × 22.5cm)
Anchor stranded cotton: one skein each of 209 green-blue, 215 emerald, 258 bright green, 288 medium yellow, 291 bright yellow, 323 peach, 1009 pale yellow

Preparation
1 Measure and mark the middle of the fabric with vertical and horizontal rows of basting stitches (refer to Better Techniques).

Size of finished embroidery:
3½ × 5in (8.75 × 12.5cm)

Working the embroidery
2 The centre of the embroidery is indicated by arrows on each side. This coincides with the basting stitches. Following the chart and the colour key, begin by embroidering the middle of the design using 3 strands of thread together. Complete as shown on the chart.

3 Define the water-lily petals in back stitch using 1 strand of 291.

Finishing
4 Remove the basting stitches. Press the finished embroidery lightly on the wrong side.

5 Mount the embroidery ready for framing (refer to Better Techniques).

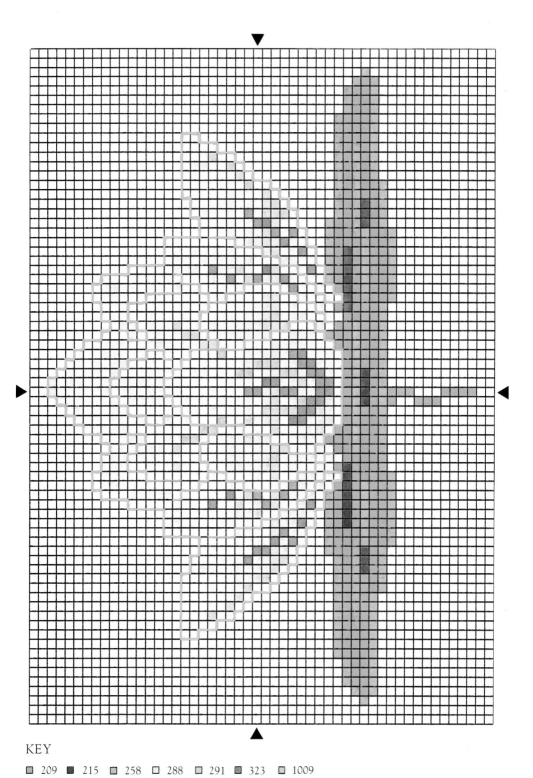

KEY

Herbal sachets

*These two herbal sachets look delightful together and each could
be filled with a different herb. Make several of these sachets to
keep wardrobes and drawers sweet smelling.*

SACHET A
Materials
2 pieces of Hardanger cream fabric 22
   holes per inch (2.5cm) size 8 × 6in
   (20 × 15cm)
Anchor stranded cotton: one skein each
   of 243 leaf green, 266 pea green, 311
   jasmine, 1025 plum, 9575 rose

Size of finished embroidery: $3\frac{3}{4} \times 4\frac{1}{4}$in (9.5 × 10.5cm)

Polyester toy stuffing
Herbs
Ribbon

KEY

- 243
- 266
- 311
- 1025
- 9575

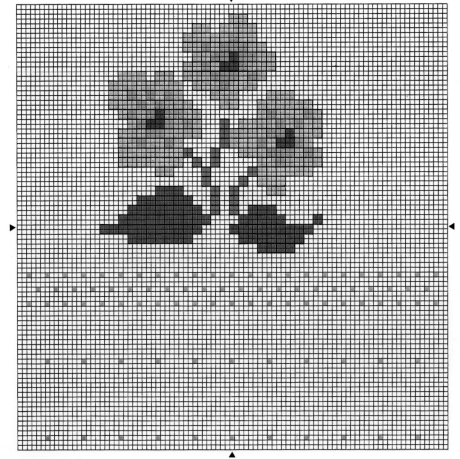

NB 4 squares on chart = 1 stitch

SACHET B

Materials

2 pieces of Hardanger cream fabric 22
  holes per inch (2.5cm) size 8 × 6in
  (20 × 15cm)
Anchor stranded cotton: one skein each
  of 243 leaf green, 266 pea green, 293
  daffodil, 1023 coral
Polyester toy stuffing
Herbs
Ribbon

Preparation

1 Measure and mark the middle of the
fabric with vertical and horizontal rows
of basting stitches (refer to Better
Techniques).

Working the embroidery

2 The centre of the chart is indicated by
arrows on each side. This coincides with
the basting stitches. Following the chart
and the colour key, begin by
embroidering the middle block of colour
using 2 strands of thread together,
working the main pattern using the cross
stitch over 2 sides. Complete the design
as shown on the chart.

Finishing

3 Remove the basting stitches. Press the
finished embroidery lightly on the back.

4 Place the two pieces of fabric together
with the embroidered sides facing, and
neatly sew together around the sides and
bottom edge. Turn right sides out.

5 Use a four-sided stitch along the top of
the sachets, and then carefully pull out
the horizontal threads to make a fringe.
Fill the sachet with the toy stuffing mixed
with herbs and tie with a pretty ribbon.

Size of finished embroidery: 3¾ × 4¼in (9.5 × 10.5cm)   NB 4 squares on chart = 1 stitch

KEY

- ◻ 243
- ◻ 266
- ◻ 293
- ◻ 1023

Floral clock

This pretty floral design is made into a clock face and will make an ideal gift for anyone who loves flowers. A timeless design that will give hours of pleasure!

Materials

1 piece of Hardanger cream fabric 22
holes per inch size 8 × 6in (20 × 15cm)
Anchor stranded cotton: one skein each
of 265 jade, 267 lime green (light), 323
peach, 1024 caramel, 1039 sapphire
Clock

Preparation

1 Measure and mark the middle of the
fabric with vertical and horizontal rows
of basting stitches (refer to Better
Techniques).

Working the embroidery

2 The centre of the chart is indicated by
arrows on each side. This coincides with
the basting stitches. Following the chart
and the colour key, begin by
embroidering the middle block of colour
using 2 strands of thread together.
Complete the design as shown on the
chart.

3 Follow the chart to stitch the flower
stems in back stitch using 1 thread of
267.

Finishing

4 Remove the basting stitches. Press the
finished embroidery lightly on the back.

Mounting

5 Mount the embroidery on the clock
following the manufacturer's
instructions.

KEY

◻ 265 ◼ 267 ◻ 323 ◼ 1024 ◻ 1039

Size of finished embroidery: 5 × 3½in (12.5 × 8.75cm)

19

Strawberries bookmark

This bookmark will be a delightful reminder of delicious strawberries every time you open your favourite recipe or gardening book. It can be worked on a larger-count fabric to make a bell-pull.

Materials
1 piece of Hardanger cream fabric 22 holes per inch (2.5cm) size 12 × 5in (30 × 12.5cm)
Anchor stranded cotton: one skein each of 1 white, 23 pink, 46 scarlet, 244 moss green, 289 sand
Piece of lining fabric, same size
Tassel

Preparation
1 Measure and mark the middle of the fabric with vertical and horizontal rows of basting stitches (refer to Better Techniques).

Working the embroidery
2 The centre of the chart is indicated by arrows on each side. This coincides with the basting stitches. Following the chart and the colour key, begin by embroidering the middle block of colour using 2 strands of thread together. Complete the design as shown on the chart.

3 Define the strawberry flowers in back stitch using 1 strand of 23. Also using back stitch, follow the chart to stitch the flower stems in 1 strand of 244.

Finishing
4 Remove the basting stitches. Press the finished embroidery lightly on the back.

5 Trim the excess fabric to within ½in (1cm) of the embroidery. To line the bookmark place the embroidery and lining fabric together, right sides facing, and neatly stitch around the edge leaving a gap along the top edge. Turn the embroidery right sides out and sew the gap together. Press and add a tassel at the bottom.

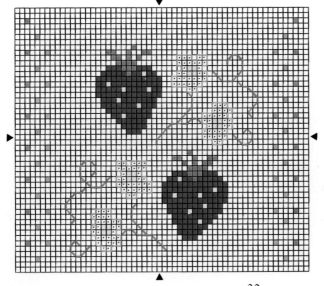

Size of finished embroidery:
7¼ × 2½in (18 × 6.25cm)

KEY

⊡	1
■	23
■	46
■	244
□	289

Spectacles case

Inspired by the Blue-eyed Susie, this charming spectacles case is quick and easy to make. Why not stitch your initials in the top left-hand corner?

Materials
2 pieces of Aida cream fabric 14 holes
  per inch (2.5cm) size 8 × 5in
  (20 × 12.5cm)

Anchor stranded cotton: one skein each
  of 131 bluebell, 243 leaf green, 293
  daffodil, 1036 navy
2 pieces of lining fabric, same size

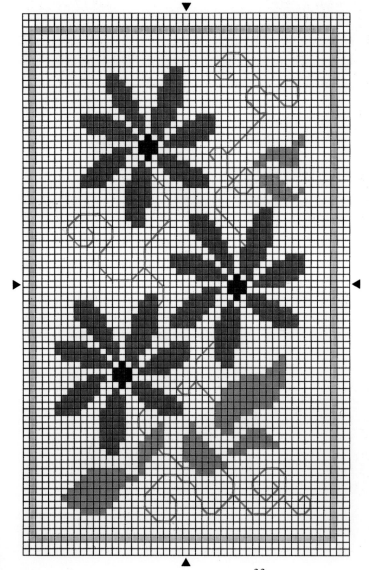

KEY
■ 131
■ 243
□ 293
■ 1036

Size of finished embroidery:
5½ × 3½in (13.75 × 8.75cm)

Preparation
1 Measure and mark the middle of the fabric with rows of horizontal and vertical basting stitches (refer to Better Techniques).

Working the embroidery
2 The centre of the chart is indicated by arrows on each side. This coincides with the basting stitches. Following the chart and the colour key, begin by embroidering the middle block of colour using 3 strands of thread together. Complete the design as shown on the chart.

3 Follow the chart to stitch the stems in back stitch using 1 thread of 243.

Finishing
4 Remove the basting stitches. Press the finished embroidery lightly on the back.

5 Place the 2 pieces of Aida fabric together with the embroidery facing inwards and neatly sew around 3 sides. Turn right sides out and press.

6 With right sides facing, sew together the lining pieces to make a pocket slightly smaller than the spectacles case. Leave the top side open. Trim seam allowances to ¼in (5mm).

7 Slip the lining inside the spectacles case and sew them together round the top edge using slip stitch.

Flower card

A pretty bunch of flowers tied with a bow makes a lovely greetings card. It does not take long to stitch and will be greatly appreciated as a 'thank-you'.

Materials

1 piece of Aida white fabric 11 holes per inch (2.5cm) size 6 × 4in (15 × 10cm)

Anchor stranded cotton: one skein each of 131 bluebell, 133 midnight, 229 bottle green, 293 daffodil, 328 apricot, 340 copper

Card mount

KEY

■	131	☐	293
■	133	■	328
■	229	■	340

Size of finished embroidery:
3¾ × 2¼in (9.5 × 5.5cm)

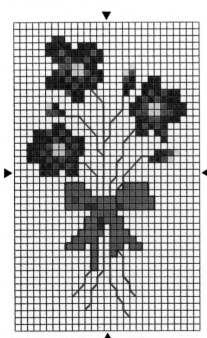

Preparation

1 Measure and mark the middle of the fabric with vertical and horizontal rows of basting stitches (refer to Better Techniques).

Working the embroidery

2 The centre of the chart is indicated by arrows on each side. This coincides with the basting stitches. Following the chart and the colour key, begin by embroidering the middle block of colour using 3 strands of thread together. Complete the design as shown on the chart.

3 Follow the chart to stitch the flower stems in back stitch using 1 thread of 229.

Finishing

4 Remove the basting stitches. Press the finished embroidery lightly on the back.

5 Trim the edges of the fabric to fit the card, leaving as much allowance as possible around the actual embroidery (refer to Better Techniques).

6 Spread glue thinly around the edges of the window on the inside of the card. Position the embroidery behind the window, and stick it down.

7 Spread glue round the edges of the left-hand panel and fold over the embroidery. Press down firmly and leave to dry thoroughly.

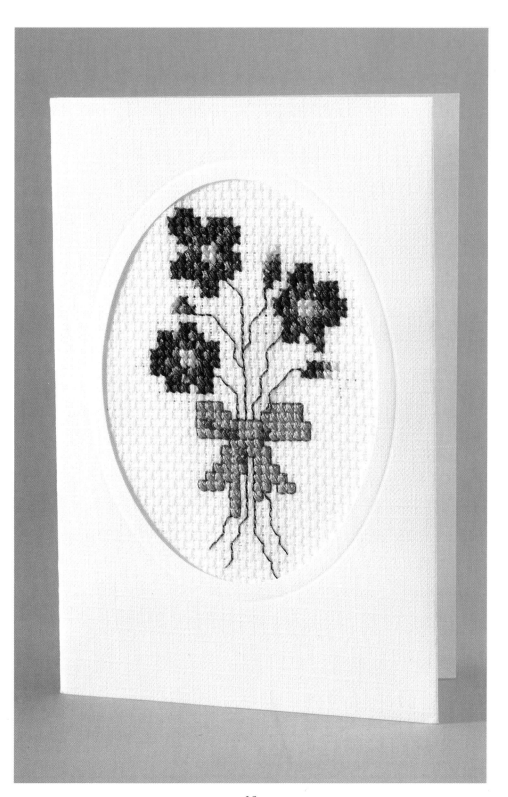

Primroses pincushion

This pretty pincushion will brighten any work-basket and could even be used as a herbal sachet if sweet-smelling herbs were added to the stuffing.

Materials

2 pieces of Aida cream fabric 14 holes per inch (2.5cm) size 5 × 5in (12.5 × 12.5cm)

Anchor stranded cotton: one skein each of 265 jade, 266 pea green, 293 daffodil, 298 honey, 1047 amber

Polyester toy stuffing

Preparation

1 Measure and mark the middle of the fabric with vertical and horizontal rows of basting stitches (refer to Better Techniques).

Working the embroidery

2 The centre of the chart is indicated by arrows on each side. This coincides with the basting stitches. Following the chart and the colour key, begin by embroidering the middle block of colour using 3 strands of thread together. Complete the design as shown on the chart.

Size of finished embroidery:
3¾ × 3¾in (9.5 × 9.5cm)

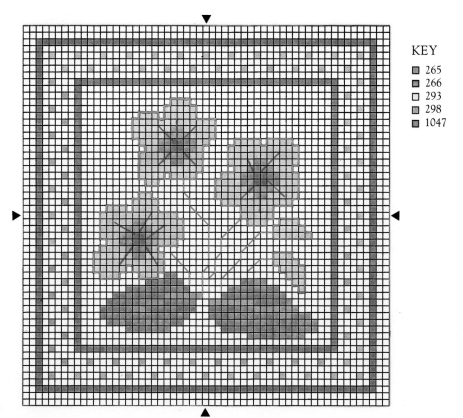

KEY

■ 265
■ 266
□ 293
■ 298
■ 1047

3 Define the edges of the flowers in back stitch using 1 thread of 298. Follow the chart to stitch the flower stamen in back stitch using 1 thread of 298 and the flower stems using 1 thread of 265.

Finishing
4 Remove the basting stitches. Press the finished embroidery lightly on the back.

5 Place the two pieces of fabric together with the embroidery facing inwards and neatly sew together, leaving a gap along one edge. Turn the embroidery right sides out and press.

6 Fill with the polyester toy stuffing and neatly sew the gap together using a slip stitch.

Forget-me-nots scissors case

Pretty little forget-me-not flowers were the inspiration for this design for a scissors case. It could just as easily be used for a handkerchief-holder.

Materials

2 pieces of Hardanger white fabric 22 holes per inch (2.5cm) size 6 × 6in (15 × 15cm)

Anchor stranded cotton: one skein each of 92 hyacinth, 131 bluebell, 215 emerald, 293 daffodil

Ribbon

2 pieces of lining fabric, same size

Preparation

1 Measure and mark the middle of the fabric with vertical and horizontal rows of basting stitches (refer to Better Techniques).

Working the embroidery

2 The centre of the chart is indicated by arrows on each side. This coincides with the basting stitches. Following the chart and the colour key, begin by embroidering the middle block of colour using 1 strand of thread. Complete the design as shown on the chart.

Size of finished embroidery:
Sides 4½in (11.5cm), base ½in (1.25cm)

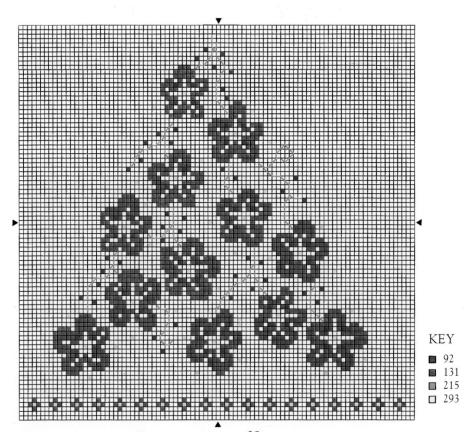

KEY

■ 92
■ 131
■ 215
□ 293

3 Follow the chart to stitch the stems in back stitch using 1 thread of 215.

Finishing

4 Remove the basting stitches. Press the finished embroidery lightly on the back.

5 Place the 2 pieces of Hardanger fabric together with the embroidery facing inwards and mark the finished shape with tacking stitches. Neatly sew around 2 long sides and the base, leaving the top edge open. Turn right sides out and press.

6 With right sides facing, sew together the lining pieces to make a pocket slightly smaller than the scissors case. Leave the top side open. Trim the seam allowances to ¼in (5mm).

7 Slip the lining into the case, and sew them together around the top edge using slip stitch. Add the ribbon.

Anemones picture

The fresh colours of anemones have been captured in this small picture. The design could be used for a small cushion by adding a border in harmonizing colours.

Materials
1 piece of Aida white fabric 14 holes per inch (2.5cm) size 6 × 8in (15 × 20cm)
Anchor stranded cotton: one skein each of 1 white, 47 claret, 92 hyacinth, 142 powder blue, 178 indigo, 244 moss green, 403 black, 1044 dark green

Preparation
1 Measure and mark the middle of the fabric with vertical and horizontal rows of basting stitches (refer to Better Techniques).

Working the embroidery
2 The centre of the chart is indicated by arrows on each side. This coincides with the basting stitches. Following the chart and the colour key, begin by embroidering the middle block of colour using 3 strands of thread together. Complete the design as shown on the chart.

3 Define the anemone petals in back stitch using 1 strand of 92.

Finishing
4 Remove the basting stitches. Press the finished embroidery lightly on the back.

5 Mount the embroidery in preparation for framing (refer to Better Techniques).

Size of finished embroidery: 3¼ × 4in (8 × 10cm)

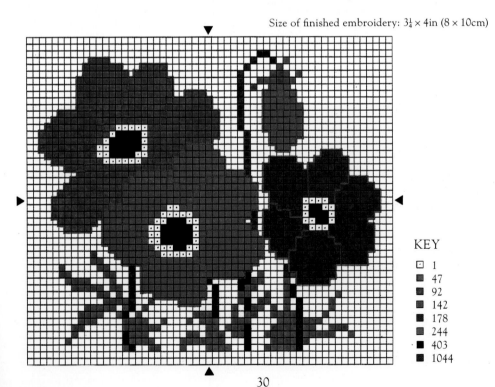

KEY
☑ 1
■ 47
■ 92
■ 142
■ 178
■ 244
·■ 403
■ 1044

Quick-mounting

Press-on adhesive board enables you to mount embroidery quickly and, later, remove it for cleaning. To use the board, peel off the protective covering and position the embroidery on the surface. Smooth in place, outwards from the centre. Fold the fabric edges to the back and tape in place.

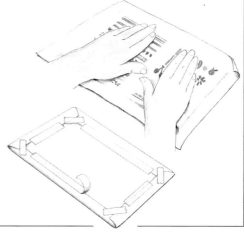

TWO

Animals and Insects

Elephant diary cover

Elephants are reputed to 'never forget' so this design is ideal as a cover for a diary or notebook. It can easily be adapted to fit any size by adding more elephants.

Materials
1 piece of Aida cream fabric 18 holes per inch (2.5cm) size 8 × 11in (20 × 27.5cm)
Anchor stranded cotton: one skein each of 59 burgundy, 146 blue, 329 orange, 388 fawn, 393 taupe

Preparation
1 Measure and mark the middle of the fabric with vertical and horizontal rows of basting stitches (refer to Better Techniques).

Working the embroidery
2 The centre of the chart is indicated by arrows on each side. This coincides with the basting stitches. Following the chart and the colour key, begin by embroidering the middle block of colour using 3 strands of thread together. Complete the design as shown on the chart.

3 Follow the chart to stitch the elephants' tusks and toes in back stitch using 1 thread of 393.

Finishing
4 Remove the basting stitches. Press the finished embroidery lightly on the back.

5 Wrap the fabric around the notebook you wish to cover with the design centred on the front.

6 Turn the raw edges to the back of the fabric, allowing 1in (2.5cm) on each vertical side and ¼in (5mm) extra on the horizontal sides, and neatly hem in place. Trim the excess fabric to ¼in (5mm) of the hem-stitch.

7 Make a pocket along each vertical side by turning the extra fabric back and catching it carefully at the top and bottom. This will hold the notebook or diary in place.

Size of finished
embroidery: $6 \times 2\frac{3}{4}$in
$(15 \times 6.75\text{cm})$

KEY
■ 59
■ 146
■ 329
■ 388
■ 393

Owl bell-pull

The three wise old owls are sitting on their branches over the tree of life. This would make a special present for someone who has just passed their exams.

Materials
1 piece of Aida cream fabric 14 holes per
  inch (2.5cm) size 17 × 6in (42.5 × 15cm)
Anchor stranded cotton: one skein each
  of 244 moss green, 347 butterscotch,
  359 mahogany, 367 stone, 370 auburn,
  403 black, 1044 dark green
Wooden bell-pull ends

Preparation
1 Measure and mark the middle of the
fabric with vertical and horizontal rows
of basting stitches (refer to Better
Techniques).

Working the embroidery
2 The centre of the chart is indicated by
arrows on each side. This coincides with
the basting stitches. Following the chart
and the colour key, begin by stitching the
middle block of colour using 3 strands of
thread together. Complete the design as
shown on the chart.

3 Follow the chart to stitch the leaf
stems in back stitch using 1 thread of
244. Follow the chart to stitch the outline
of the tree and the branches in back
stitch using 1 thread of 359.

Finishing
4 Remove the basting stitches. Press the
finished embroidery lightly on the back.

5 Turn the side edges of the fabric to the
back and hem neatly. Trim excess fabric
to within ¼in (5mm) of the hem stitches.

6 Attach the top and bottom ends of the
bell-pull by folding the edges of the fabric
over the wooden ends and catching the
fabric with a few stitches at each side.

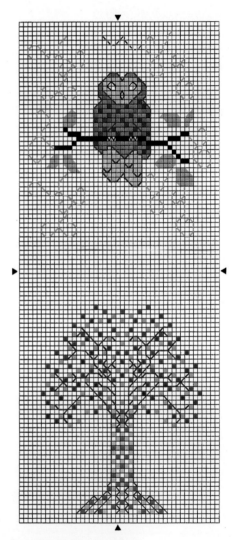

Size of finished embroidery:
11½ × 3in (28.75 × 7.5cm)

KEY

▪ 244	▫ 367	▪ 1044
▪ 347	▪ 370	
▪ 359	▪ 403	

36

37

Honeybees picture

Bees are always a reminder of hot summer days, and this picture would be an ideal keepsake for someone who loves to cook and to make jam.

Materials
1 piece of Aida cream fabric 11 holes per inch (2.5cm) size 14 × 6in (35 × 15cm)
Anchor stranded cotton: one skein each of 298 honey, 403 black, 1002 marmalade, 1010 blush, 1041 granite

Preparation
1 Measure and mark the middle of the fabric with vertical and horizontal rows of basting stitches (refer to Better Techniques).

Working the embroidery
2 The centre of the chart is indicated by arrows on each side. This coincides with the basting stitches. Following the chart and the colour key, begin by embroidering the middle block of colour using 3 strands of thread together. Complete the design as shown on the chart.

3 Follow the chart to stitch the bees' wings in back stitch using 1 thread of 403. Follow the chart to stitch the bees' legs and antennae using 2 threads of 403. Follow the chart to stitch the honeycombs using 2 threads of 298.

Finishing
4 Remove the basting stitches. Press the finished embroidery lightly on the back.

5 Mount the embroidery ready for framing (refer to Better Techniques).

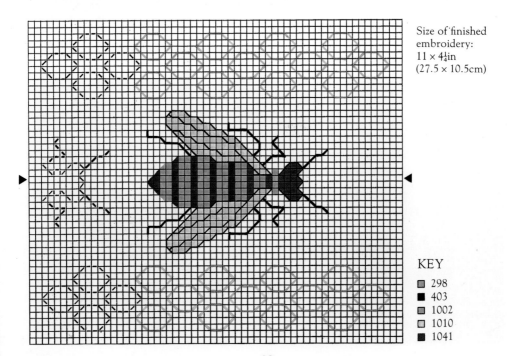

Size of finished embroidery:
11 × 4¼in
(27.5 × 10.5cm)

KEY
■ 298
■ 403
■ 1002
□ 1010
■ 1041

Flowers and cat card

This is ideal for someone who has just moved home or is recovering from an operation. Or you could give it to a friend who loves cats and flowers!

Materials
1 piece Hardanger white fabric 22 holes per inch (2.5cm) 6 × 4in (15 × 10cm)
Anchor stranded cotton: one skein each of 265 jade, 293 daffodil, 323 peach, 1007 dark brown, 1010 blush, 1025 plum
Card mount

Preparation
1 Measure and mark the middle of the fabric with vertical and horizontal rows of basting stitches (refer to Better Techniques).

Working the embroidery
2 The centre of the chart is indicated by arrows on the edges. This coincides with the basting stitches. Following the chart and the colour key, begin by embroidering the middle block of colour using 2 strands of thread together, stitching the design over 2 holes. Complete the design as shown on the chart.

3 Follow the chart to stitch an outline around the cat in back stitch using 1 thread of 1007. Stitch the cat's whiskers in 293, the leaves in 265 and the table leg

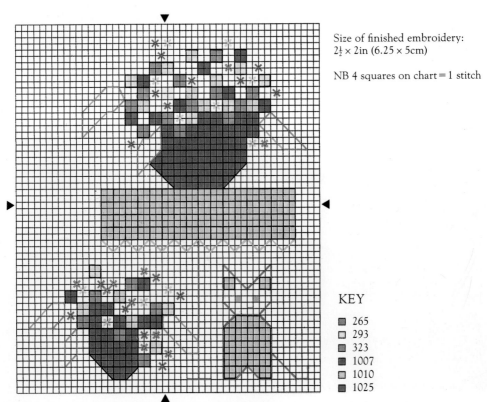

Size of finished embroidery:
2½ × 2in (6.25 × 5cm)

NB 4 squares on chart = 1 stitch

KEY

- ■ 265
- □ 293
- ▨ 323
- ■ 1007
- □ 1010
- ▨ 1025

40

in 1025, in back stitch. The cat's eyes are stitched in a small cross stitch using 1 thread of 265.

4 Mix cross stitches and french knots to create the textured effect in the flower baskets.

Finishing
5 Remove the basting stitches. Press the finished embroidery lightly on the back.

6 Trim the edges of the fabric to fit the card, leaving as much allowance as possible around the actual embroidery (refer to Better Techniques).

7 Spread glue thinly around the edges of the window on the inside of the card. Position the embroidery behind the window and stick it down.

8 Spread glue around the edges of the left-hand panel and fold it over the embroidery. Press down firmly and leave to dry thoroughly.

41

Butterfly picture

This picture will brighten any child's room and will be a reminder of days spent chasing butterflies in the garden. A pink, yellow or orange mount can be used to match any bedroom interior.

Materials
1 piece of Aida cream fabric 14 holes per inch (2.5cm) size 5 × 7in (12.5 × 17.5cm)
Anchor stranded cotton: one skein each of 46 scarlet, 302 straw, 304 tangerine, 328 apricot, 352 chestnut, 403 black, 410 aquamarine

Preparation
1 Measure and mark the middle of the fabric with vertical and horizontal rows of basting stitches (refer to Better Techniques).

Working the embroidery
2 The centre of the chart is indicated by arrows on each side. This coincides with the basting stitches. Following the chart and the colour key, begin by embroidering the middle block of colour using 3 strands of thread together. Complete the design as shown on the chart.

3 Follow the chart to stitch the butterfly's antennae in back stitch using 1 thread of 403. Also use 1 thread of 403 to outline in back stitch the line where the wings meet.

Finishing
4 Remove the basting stitches. Press the finished embroidery lightly on the back.

5 Mount the embroidery ready for framing (refer to Better Techniques).

Size of finished embroidery: 3 × 4in (7.5 × 10cm)

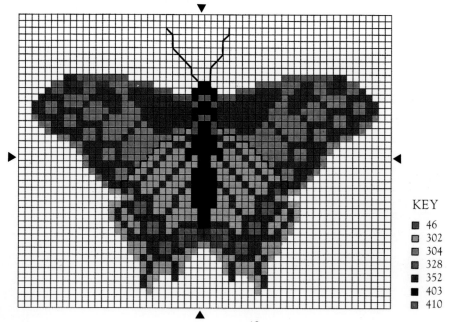

KEY
■ 46
□ 302
□ 304
■ 328
■ 352
■ 403
■ 410

Butterfly cushion
This design can also be used for a
cushion cover. Work the design on a
piece of fabric measuring 18 × 18in
(45 × 45cm). Find the centre of the
fabric and start by embroidering the
central butterfly, positioning the
other butterflies as shown. Use a
piece of fabric the same size for the
back of the cushion cover. Place the
two pieces of fabric right sides
together and sew around 3 sides.
Turn right side out and press. Insert a
cushion pad and sew up the last side.

Ladybird spectacles case

The bright red ladybirds are a cheerful colour and will always make you smile when you use the spectacles case. Ideal for ordinary glasses and sun-glasses.

Materials

1 piece of Aida cream fabric 18 holes per inch (2.5cm) size 9 × 5in (22.5 × 12.5cm)

Anchor stranded cotton: one skein each of 46 scarlet, 239 olive green (dark), 266 pea green, 379 cinnamon, 403 black, 1020 damask

Felt for backing, same size

2 pieces of lining fabric, same size

Preparation

1 Measure and mark the middle of the fabric with vertical and horizontal rows of basting stitches (refer to Better Techniques).

Working the embroidery

2 The centre of the chart is indicated by arrows on each side. This coincides with the basting stitches. Following the chart and the colour key, begin by stitching the middle block of colour using 2 strands of thread together. Complete the design as shown on the chart.

3 Follow the chart to stitch down the centre of each ladybird in back stitch using 1 thread of 403.

Finishing

4 Remove the basting stitches. Press the finished embroidery lightly on the back. Trim the fabric back to within ½in (1cm) around the two sides and bottom edge. Fold the top edge to the back leaving ¼in (5mm) fabric showing above the design.

5 Place the embroidery and felt together, right sides facing, and neatly sew together along the 2 sides and bottom edge. Trim excess fabric and cut across the corners. Turn right sides out and press.

6 With right sides facing, sew together the lining pieces to make a pocket slightly smaller than the case. Leave the top open. Trim seam allowances to ¼in (5mm). Slip the lining inside the case and sew together around the top using slip stitch.

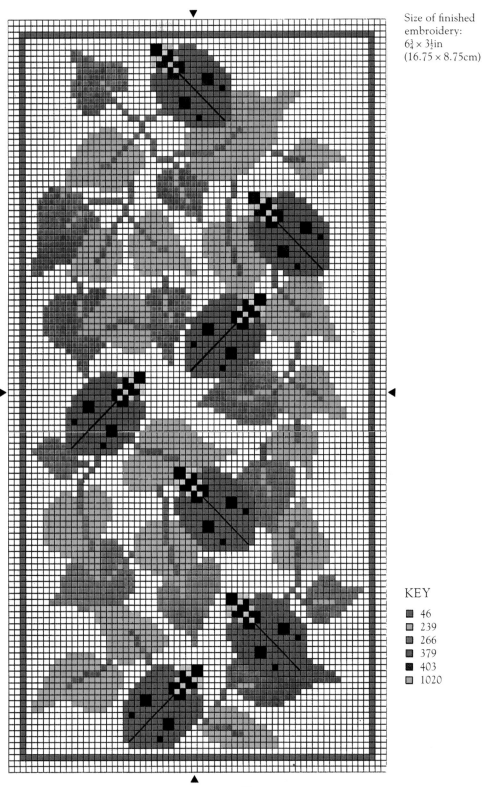

Size of finished
embroidery:
$6\frac{3}{4} \times 3\frac{1}{2}$in
$(16.75 \times 8.75$cm$)$

KEY

- 46
- 239
- 266
- 379
- 403
- 1020

Bunny card

This cuddly bunny makes a lovely card for a child. If they have a pet rabbit, why not stitch its name across the bottom to make it extra special?

Materials

1 piece of Aida white fabric 14 holes per inch (2.5cm) size 4 × 4in (10 × 10cm)

Anchor stranded cotton: one skein each of 242 green, 301 blonde, 376 pale brown, small length of 403 black, 885 ivory, 1007 dark brown

Card mount

Preparation

1 Measure and mark the middle of the fabric with vertical and horizontal rows of basting stitches (refer to Better Techniques).

Working the embroidery

2 The centre of the chart is indicated by arrows on each side. This coincides with the basting stitches. Following the chart and the colour key, begin by stitching the middle block of colour using 3 strands of thread together. Complete the design as shown on the chart.

3 Stitch the yellow flowers using a french knot in 301.

Finishing

4 Remove the basting stitches. Press the finished embroidery lightly on the back. Trim the edges of the fabric to fit the card, leaving as much allowance as possible around the actual embroidery.

5 Spread glue thinly around the edges of the window on the inside of the card. Position the embroidery behind the window and stick it down.

6 Spread glue round the edges of the left-hand panel and fold over the embroidery. Press down firmly and leave to dry.

Size of finished embroidery:
$2\frac{1}{2} \times 2\frac{1}{2}$in (6.25 × 6.25cm)

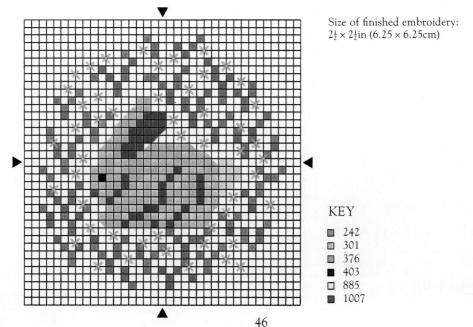

KEY

- ▨ 242
- ▨ 301
- ▨ 376
- ■ 403
- ☐ 885
- ▨ 1007

Sheep picture

If you have just returned from a holiday on or near a farm, why not embroider this little picture as a lasting reminder of a happy time?

Materials
1 piece of Aida cream fabric 14 holes per inch (2.5cm) size 5 × 7in (12.5 × 17.5cm)
Anchor stranded cotton: one skein each of 1 white, 239 green (dark), 254 green (pale), 291 bright yellow, 300 pale yellow, 311 jasmine, 329 orange, 371 brown

Preparation
1 Measure and mark the middle of the fabric with vertical and horizontal rows of basting stitches (refer to better Techniques).

Working the embroidery
2 The centre of the chart is indicated by arrows on each side. This coincides with the basting stitches. Following the chart and the colour key, begin by embroidering the middle block of colour using 3 strands of thread together. Complete the design as shown on the chart.

Finishing
3 Remove the basting stitches. Press the finished embroidery lightly on the back.

4 Mount the embroidery ready for framing (refer to Better Techniques).

Size of finished
embroidery:
$2 \times 3\frac{3}{4}$in
$(5 \times 9.5\text{cm})$

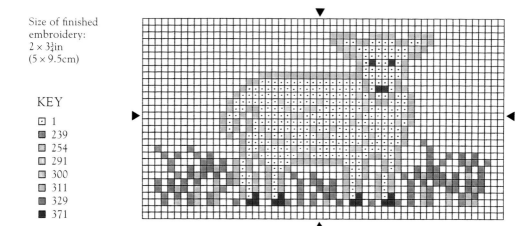

KEY

- ⊡ 1
- ■ 239
- ☐ 254
- ☐ 291
- ☐ 300
- ☐ 311
- ☐ 329
- ■ 371

THREE

Special Occasions

Geometric pincushion

*This makes an ideal birthday present for a keen embroiderer. It is
unusual to find a pincushion in a wooden mount and it will,
therefore, be appreciated for many years.*

Materials

1 piece Aida white fabric 18 holes per
inch (2.5cm) size 6 × 6in (15 × 15cm)
Anchor stranded cotton: one skein each
of 38 cerise, 225 tree green, 230 dark
green
Wooden pincushion mount

KEY
■ 38
□ 225
■ 230

Size of finished embroidery: 4 × 4in (10 × 10cm)

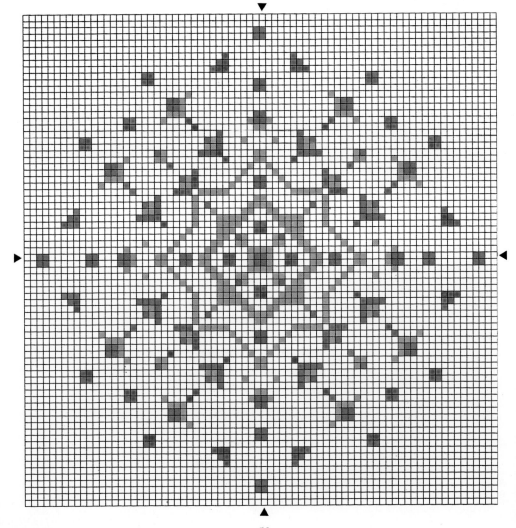

52

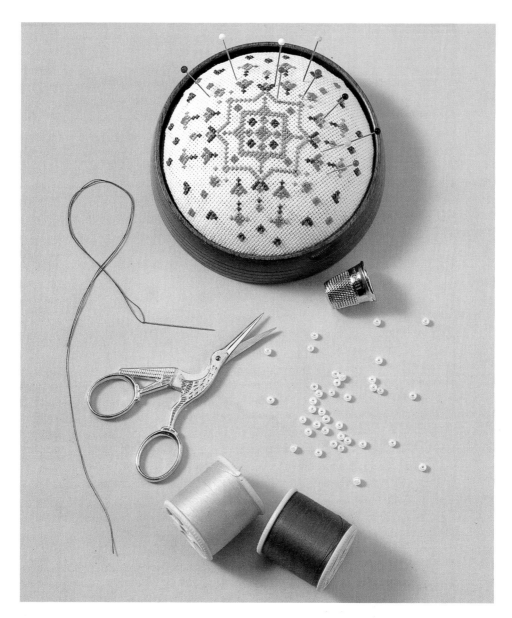

Preparation

1 Measure and mark the middle of the fabric with vertical and horizontal rows of basting stitches (refer to Better Techniques).

Working the embroidery

2 The centre of the chart is indicated by arrows on each side. This coincides with the basting stitches. Following the chart and the colour key, begin by stitching the middle block of colour using 3 strands of thread together. Complete the design as shown on the chart.

Finishing

3 Remove the basting stitches. Press the finished embroidery lightly on the back.

4 To mount the embroidery, remove the pad from the frame, cover it with the embroidery and push it back into place.

Engagement cushion

A quick little cushion to make that can be filled with lots of your favourite herbs and spices. With its heart motif it will be a special gift for a bride-to-be.

Materials

2 pieces Aida cream fabric 14 holes per inch (2.5cm) size 8 × 8in (20 × 20cm)

4 pieces Aida cream fabric 14 holes per inch (2.5cm) size 8 × 2in (20 × 5cm)

Anchor stranded cotton: one skein each of 1006 cherry, 1023 coral, 1030 lavender

Polyester toy stuffing

Scented herbs (optional)

Size of finished embroidery: 5¾ × 5¾in (14.25 × 14.25cm)

Preparation

1 Measure and mark the middle of the fabric with vertical and horizontal rows of basting stitches (refer to Better Techniques).

KEY

■ 1006
□ 1023
■ 1030

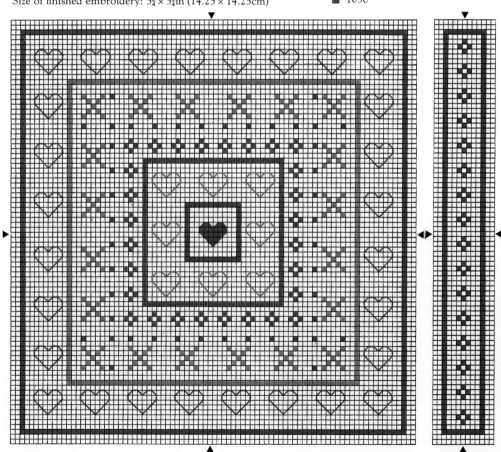

Working the embroidery

2 The centre of the chart is indicated by arrows on each side. This coincides with the basting stitches. Following the chart and the colour key, begin by embroidering the middle block of colour using 3 strands of thread together. Complete the design as shown on the chart. Stitch the 4 side panels following the chart.

3 Follow the chart to stitch the pink and red hearts in back stitch using 1 thread of 1023 and 1006 respectively.

Finishing

4 Remove the basting stitches. Press the finished embroidery lightly on the back.

5 With right sides facing sew the 4 side panels neatly to the sides of the main embroidery panel. Turn right sides out and press.

6 Neatly sew the 4 pieces together at the corner edges.

7 With right sides facing sew the back panel to the 4 side panels, leaving a gap along one edge. Turn right sides out and press.

8 Fill with the toy stuffing, adding scented herbs if required, and neatly sew the gap together.

Christening alphabet picture

This alphabet picture makes a wonderful christening present. It can be made using any letter of the alphabet and its recipient will treasure it forever.

Materials

1 piece Hardanger ecru 22 holes per inch (2.5cm) size 5 × 5in (12.5 × 12.5cm)
Anchor stranded cotton: one skein each of 243 leaf green, 293 daffodil, 1044 dark green, 1047 amber, 5975 red-brown

Preparation

1 Measure and mark the middle of the fabric with vertical and horizontal rows of basting stitches (refer to Better Techniques).

Working the embroidery

2 The centre of the chart is indicated by arrows on each side. This coincides with the basting stitches. Following the chart and the colour key, begin by embroidering the middle block of colour using 2 strands of thread together. Complete the design as shown on the chart..

3 Follow the chart to stitch the flower stems in back stitch using 1 thread of 1044.

Finishing

4 Remove the basting stitches. Press the finished embroidery lightly on the back.

5 Mount the embroidery ready for framing (refer to Better Techniques).

Size of finished embroidery:
2¼ × 2½in (5.5 × 6.25cm)

KEY

■ 243 □ 293 ■ 1044 ▨ 1047 ■ 5975

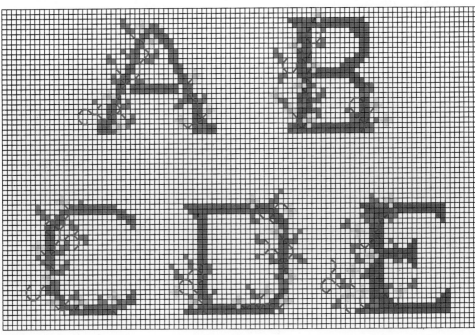

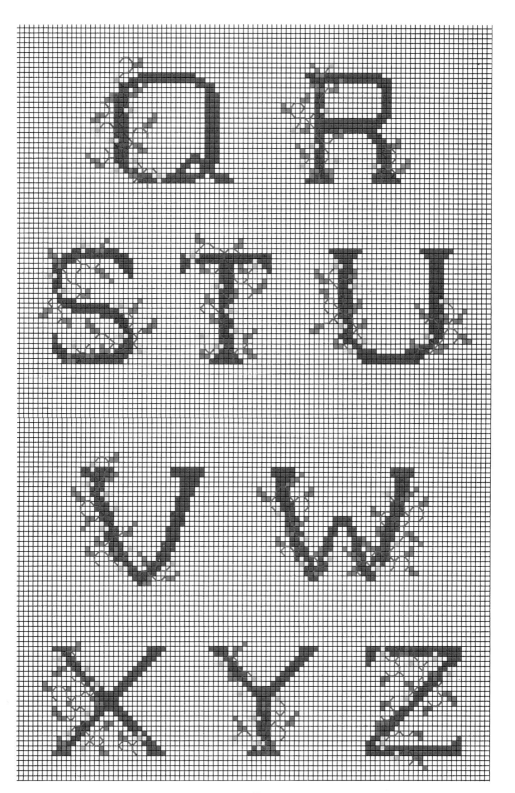

House-warming candle screen

This delightful keepsake makes an excellent and unusual house-warming present. It can be used all year round or just at Christmas time.

Materials
1 piece Aida cream fabric 18 holes per inch (2.5cm) size 8 × 6in (20 × 15cm)
Anchor stranded cotton: one skein each of 47 claret, 258 bright green, 295 sunshine, 363 mustard
Candle screen

Size of finished embroidery: 5 × 3in (12.5 × 7.5cm)

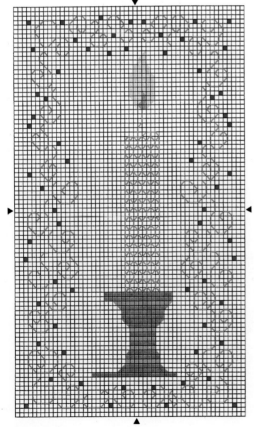

Preparation
1 Measure and mark the middle of the fabric with vertical and horizontal rows of basting stitches (refer to Better Techniques).

Working the embroidery
2 The centre of the chart is indicated by arrows on each side. This coincides with the basting stitches. Following the chart and the colour key, begin by embroidering the middle block of colour using 2 strands of thread together. Complete the design as shown on the chart.

3 Follow the chart to stitch the candle honeycomb in back stitch using 1 thread of 363. Follow the chart to work the green border detail in back stitch using 1 thread of 258.

Finishing
4 Remove the basting stitches. Press the finished embroidery lightly on the back.

5 Mount in the candle screen following the manufacturer's instructions.

KEY

■ 47
■ 258
□ 295
□ 363

Christmas bell decoration

A beautiful sparkling bell in bright, cheerful colours that will last for years and years and remain fresh and appealing each time you look at it.

Materials
1 piece Aida white blockweave fabric 18 holes per inch (2.5cm) size 6 × 4½in (15 × 11.25cm)
Anchor stranded cotton: one skein each of 29 poppy, 229 bottle green, 289 sand, 329 orange, one reel of Kreinik 027
Bell mount and frame

Preparation
1 Measure and mark the middle of the fabric with vertical and horizontal rows of basting stitches (refer to Better Techniques).

Working the embroidery
2 The centre of the chart is indicated by arrows on each side. This coincides with the basting stitches. Following the chart

Size of finished embroidery: 3¼ × 3in (8 × 7.5cm)

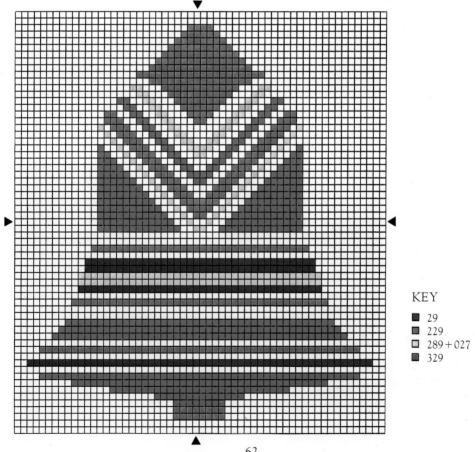

KEY
- ■ 29
- ■ 229
- □ 289 + 027
- ■ 329

and the colour key, begin by embroidering the middle block of colour using 2 strands of thread together. Add Kreinik 027 thread to the orange areas where you want to add a bit of variety. Complete the design as shown on the chart.

Finishing

3 Remove the basting stitches. Press the finished embroidery lightly on the back.

4 Glue the embroidery to the cardboard mount of the bell, trim away excess fabric and place in the silver bell frame.

Christmas tree decorations

These are so easy to make that several can be stitched in one evening. They can be made in different colours to create striking features on the Christmas tree.

Christmas tree

Materials
1 piece Aida white fabric 18 holes per
   inch (2.5cm) size 4 × 4in (10 × 10cm)
Anchor stranded cotton: one skein each
   of 29 poppy, 225 tree green, 291 bright
   yellow, 359 mahogany
Felt backing, same size
Polyester toy stuffing
Ribbon

Snowman

Materials
1 piece Aida cream fabric 18 holes per
   inch (2.5cm) size 4 × 4in (10 × 10cm)
Anchor stranded cotton: one skein each
   of 1 white, 29 poppy, 225 tree green,
   291 bright yellow, 359 mahogany, 403
   black
Felt backing
Polyester toy stuffing
Ribbon

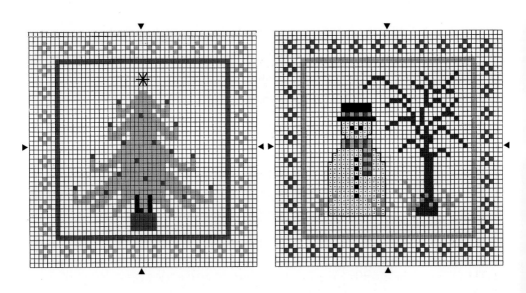

Size of finished embroideries: 2¾ × 2¾in (6.75 × 6.75cm)

KEY

■ 29	■ 291
■ 225	■ 359

KEY

⊡ 1	■ 225	■ 359
■ 29	■ 291	■ 403

Preparation
1 Measure and mark the middle of the
fabric with vertical and horizontal rows
of basting stitches (refer to Better
Techniques).

Working the embroidery
2 The centre of the chart is indicated by
arrows on each side. This coincides with
the basting stitches. Following the chart
and the colour key, begin by
embroidering the middle block of colour
using 2 strands of thread together.
Complete the design as shown on the
chart.

3 **Christmas tree:** Follow the chart to
stitch the star in back stitch using 2

strands of 291. **Snowman:** Follow the
chart to stitch an outline around the
snowman in back stitch using 1 thread of
403.

Finishing
4 Remove the basting stitches. Press the
finished embroidery lightly on the back.

5 Place the felt backing and embroidery
together with the embroidery facing
inwards and neatly sew together leaving a
gap along one edge. Trim the corners
diagonally, turn right sides out and press.

6 Fill with the toy stuffing and sew the
gap together using slip stitch. Add a
ribbon at the top.

Valentine's card

A special valentine's card for a loved one. It is easy to make and will be a keepsake for a lifetime. The person's initials or name could be stitched in the centre.

Materials

1 piece of Aida white fabric 14 holes per inch (2.5cm) size 4 × 4in (10 × 10cm)

Anchor stranded cotton: one skein each of 47 claret, 50 salmon, 229 bottle green, 293 daffodil

Card mount

Preparation

1 Measure and mark the middle of the fabric with vertical and horizontal rows of basting stitches (refer to Better Techniques).

Working the embroidery

2 The centre of the chart is indicated by arrows on each side. This coincides with the basting stitches. Following the chart and the colour key, begin by embroidering the middle block of colour using 3 strands of thread together. Complete the design as shown on the chart.

3 Follow the chart to stitch the green in the centre of the design in back stitch using 1 thread of 229. Outline the heart in back stitch using 1 thread of 47.

Size of finished embroidery: 2½ × 2½in (6.25 × 6.25cm)

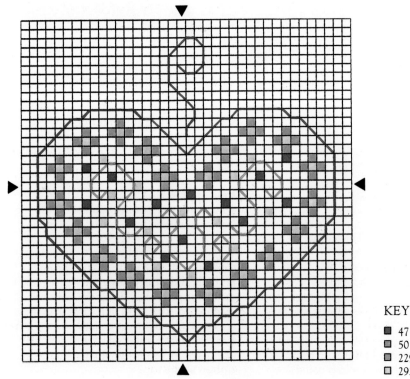

KEY
- ■ 47
- ▨ 50
- ▨ 229
- □ 293

Finishing

4 Remove the basting stitches. Press the finished embroidery lightly on the back.

5 Trim the edges of the fabric to fit the card, leaving as much allowance as possible around the actual embroidery (refer to Better Techniques).

6 Spread glue thinly around the edges of the window on the inside of the card. Position the embroidery behind the window and stick it down.

7 Spread glue round the edges of the left-hand panel and fold it over the embroidery. Press down firmly and leave to dry thoroughly.

Baby birth card

A special card to congratulate the parents of a new-born baby. The little pram has been stitched in blue here, but could easily be done in pink.

Materials
1 piece Aida white fabric 14 holes per inch (2.5cm) size 5 × 4in (12.5 × 10cm)
Anchor stranded cotton: one skein each of 55 shell pink, 98 purple, 301 blonde, 328 apricot, 1038 gentian
Card mount

Preparation
1 Measure and mark the middle of the fabric with vertical and horizontal rows of basting stitches (refer to Better Techniques).

Size of finished embroidery: 3 × 2in (7.5 × 5cm)

Working the embroidery
2 The centre of the chart is indicated by arrows on each side. This coincides with the basting stitches. Following the chart and the colour key, begin by embroidering the middle block of colour using 3 strands of thread together. Complete the design as shown on the chart.

3 Using back stitch, follow the chart to stitch the details on the pram using 1 thread of 98.

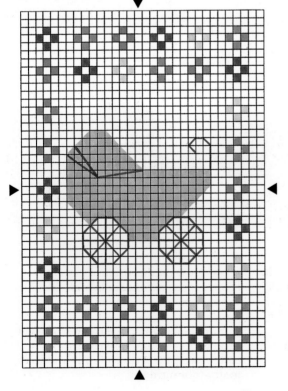

KEY
- ☐ 55
- ▨ 98
- ☐ 301
- ▨ 328
- ☐ 1038

Finishing

4 Remove the basting stitches. Press the finished embroidery lightly on the back.

5 Trim the edges of the fabric to fit the card, leaving as much allowance as possible around the actual embroidery (refer to Better Techniques).

6 Spread glue thinly around the edges of the window on the inside of the card. Position the embroidery behind the window and stick it down.

7 Spread glue around the edges of the left-hand panel and fold it over the embroidery. Press down firmly and leave to dry thoroughly.

House sampler picture

An ideal keepsake of your new home, or even the home from which you have just moved! The house name or the name of your street can be stitched on the embroidery.

Materials
1 piece evenweave ecru fabric 27 holes per inch (2.5cm) size 9 × 8in (22.5 × 20cm)

Anchor stranded cotton: one skein each of 137 peacock, 265 jade, 359 mahogany, 1007 walnut, 1025 plum, 5975 red-brown, 9525 natural

Preparation
1 Measure and mark the middle of the fabric with vertical and horizontal rows of basting stitches (refer to Better Techniques).

Working the embroidery
2 The centre of the chart is indicated by arrows on each side. This coincides with the basting stitches. Following the chart and the colour key, begin by embroidering the middle block of colour using 2 strands of thread together. Complete the design as shown on the chart.

3 Follow the chart to stitch the windows and detail on the birds in back stitch using 1 thread of 359.

Finishing

4 Remove the basting stitches. Press the finished embroidery lightly on the back.

5 Mount the embroidery ready for framing (refer to Better Techniques).

Size of finished embroidery: 7 × 5¼in (17.5 × 13cm)

KEY

■	137	▨	1025
▨	265	■	5975
■	359	▨	9525
■	1007		

Better Techniques

❦

This chapter contains advice and tips on all aspects of cross stitch – choosing threads and fabrics, setting up a frame, building up areas of colour and following a chart.

BASIC TOOLS AND EQUIPMENT
Very little basic equipment is required to enable you to produce stunning cross stitch designs. This chapter will give advice on choosing the right tools for the projects shown in this book.

Scissors
For cutting fabric to the correct size, sharp dressmaker's scissors will be required, while for general embroidery a pair of fine, pointed and very sharp embroidery scissors is essential.

Always keep your scissors for the purpose for which they were designed. Cutting paper will quickly blunt the blades. Never use unpicking tools for embroidery work as these can rip the ground threads of the fabric.

Needles
Round-ended tapestry needles are most suitable for working on evenweave fabrics. These will pass easily through the holes in the fabric without snagging or splitting the threads. Split threads will result in distorted stitches, which will not lie correctly. Tapestry needles are available in sizes 13 to 26. A size 22 needle is best for most projects in this book.

For basting and finishing projects, a range of sharp sewing needles will be required. Needles should never be left in the fabric as they can cause the threads to distort and may leave a permanent stain.

Pins
Always use stainless steel pins for your work. Discard any that are bent or rusty and never leave pins in fabric for too long, as this can leave marks that will be difficult to remove.

Measuring aids
An accurate tape measure or ruler is essential for measuring and cutting fabric. When buying a new measure, make sure it shows both inches and centimetres and remember that cloth measuring tapes stretch with use. Check your tape measure against a ruler to ensure that the measurements are still accurate and replace it if necessary.

Thimbles
Many people find it helpful to work with a thimble. However, if you are not one of these, a piece of sticking plaster over the middle finger can help to prevent soreness caused by the end of the needle.

THREADS AND YARN
Most needlework shops stock a wide range of colours and types of thread. Choose the type suited to the kind of embroidery you are working and the effect you wish to achieve.

Stranded cotton
This is formed from six strands loosely twisted together. These strands can be separated and used individually for finer

work or used in different combinations. As a general guide, on 10 to 16 count fabric use 2 or 3 strands, on 16 to 24 count use 2 strands and on 24 to 36 count use 1 strand. Stranded cotton works well in most types of embroidery.

Danish flower thread
This is a matte-finish thread made of combed cotton. On counts of 14 to 20 use 2 threads, on counts of 20 or more use 1 thread.

Soft embroidery cotton (coton à broder)
This is a dull-surfaced, 5-ply thread, usually used on heavier fabrics.

Perlé (pearl) cotton
This is a glossy, twisted 2-ply thread that comes in three thicknesses. It is ideal for embroidery on coarse (low-count) fabrics.

Crewel wool
A fine, 2-ply wool, this is used both in fine canvas embroidery and for surface stitchery on fabric.

Tapestry wool
This is a tightly twisted 4-ply yarn. It is available in a wide range of colours and is colour-fast. Usually used for canvaswork, tapestry wool can be divided into single strands for other types of embroidery.

FABRICS
Evenweave fabric
This is the most popular fabric for cross stitch. It is so named because the number of warp and weft threads in a measured inch (2.5cm) is exactly the same. It can be obtained in a variety of sizes (thread counts), types and a range of pale colours. The highest-number thread count denotes the finest weave and will, therefore, produce the smallest stitches. Fabrics range from 10 threads to the inch to 36 threads to the inch.

Hardanger is a type of evenweave fabric in which the pairs of threads are woven together. This fabric is ideal for counted-thread techniques, including cross stitch and blackwork embroidery, as the threads are easily counted and the embroidery remains firm during use.

Aida is an evenweave fabric in which the warp and weft threads have been grouped together. This creates clearly defined holes through which the needle can pass.

Binca or Bincarette is the name given to evenweave fabric with a count of 10 threads to the inch. Cross stitch worked on this is large and bold and is, therefore, suitable for children who are learning embroidery.

Plain-weave fabrics
These do not have the characteristics of evenweave, but some types can be used for counted-thread embroidery. Generally, plain-weave fabrics have a smooth, tightly woven surface and the number of threads in the warp and weft are not always the same. This category includes cotton, cotton and polyester mixes, muslin, organdie, fine embroidery linen and speciality fabrics such as hessian and hopsacking. Plain weave is most suitable for surface, free-style work.

PREPARING FABRIC
If the fabric is creased in any way, particularly along the centre fold line, it is advisable to steam-iron thoroughly before cutting or beginning to embroider. Evenweave fabric tends to fray on cut edges, so either turn and baste a hem or bind the fabric edges with masking tape.

Before starting to embroider, the exact middle of the fabric must be located by carefully counting the threads along one side, then along the adjacent side to find the centres. Mark the half-way points with pins, then work lines of coloured basting thread running from top to bottom and then across. Where the two lines of threads cross is the centre point.

When working with a very fine fabric, measure and mark the middle of the sides with pins then work lines of basting stitches between the pins.

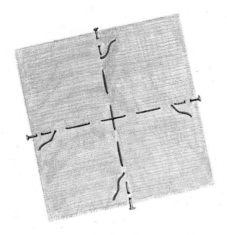

Work basting stitches top to bottom, then across.

Some embroidery fabrics are given a finishing dressing before they leave the manufacturer. This can make them feel fairly stiff to handle. You may want to wash this away before beginning to embroider, although the stiffness of the fabric can help to give your work an even tension.

EMBROIDERY FRAMES

In order to produce even, high-quality cross stitch it is essential to work with a frame. A correctly framed evenweave fabric enables the needleworker to work neatly and smoothly and the finished results will more than justify the time and initial effort required.

Experience will show which frame is best suited to a particular piece of work, but in general, small motifs are most quickly and easily worked in a round, tambour frame, while larger, more elaborate pieces are better in rectangular or slate frames.

Stretcher frames are simply four pieces of wood joined at the corners. To attach the fabric, mark the middle of each side of the frame. Mark the centre of the fabric with basting stitches. Line up the marks and fix the fabric with staples or

drawing pins. Old picture frames can also be used as a kind of stretcher frame.

Tambour or ring frames

A tambour frame consists of two rings, the outer of which has a screw fitting. This is tightened to enable the ring to hold the fabric firmly in place. Frames can be made of wood or plastic.

Tambour frames are available in several sizes from tiny 4in (10cm) diameter embroidery rings to large quilting hoops of 15in (38cm) diameter.

Framing up tambour frames

1 Separate the two rings of the frame. Place the fabric to be embroidered over the smaller ring and fit the larger ring over this, making sure that the marked centre is in the middle of the frame.
2 Smooth the fabric out evenly and straighten the grain as you tighten the outer ring, pull the fabric gently from time to time to obtain an even and firm surface.

Pull the fabric edges gently for an even surface.

When working with slippery or delicate fabrics, it is advisable to bind the smaller ring with thin, cotton tape before assembling. This will help to hold the fabric more firmly and prevents damage to fine fabric.

At the end of each session, loosen the screw and remove the larger ring. Cover the worked embroidery with tissue to protect it. Replace the ring without screwing down tightly. At the next session tighten the screw then tear the paper away over the embroidery.

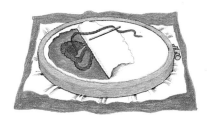

Protect partly-worked embroidery with tissue.

Rotating frames

These frames are composed of two top rollers or bars, with tapes attached and two side sections. The rollers slot into the side pieces and are held securely by pegs or butterfly-screws. The tape length regulates the size of the frame and they vary from 12in (30cm) to 27in (68cm).

Framing up rotating frames

It is essential to allow at least an extra 1in (2.5cm) on all sides when buying or cutting the fabric. Baste a single hem on the top and bottom edges of the fabric. Oversew 1in (2.5cm)-wide strong tape down each side.

Working from the centre outwards, oversew the top and bottom hemmed edges to the roller tapes, using a strong thread and small stitches. Fit the rollers into the side pieces. Turn the rollers until the fabric is taut. Tighten the butterfly screws (or insert the pegs).

Thread a darning needle with strong thread and firmly lace the side edges to the side pieces. Oversew several times at each end and wrap the thread around the rollers before finishing. Tighten the lacings occasionally as you work and slacken them off between sessions.

Embroidery rings are useful when working small areas as a tiny piece of fabric can be stitched onto a larger calico square before stretching it in the frame. Once the frame is set up, the calico behind the area to be embroidered is cut away carefully, using fine, sharp scissors.

MAKING A START

If working cross stitch for the first time, choose a design that is not too complex. A small design with only a few colours is best. Work with good-quality fabric and colour-fast threads.

It is advisable to work in a comfortable chair in a good light. This is particularly important when using higher-count fabrics and several shades of colour. An overhead lamp is useful, particularly if it is fitted with a daylight simulation bulb. This will reduce eye strain and allow the correct colour matching of threads.

The best cross stitch embroidery has clearly defined stitches that cover the ground fabric well and look crisp and sharp. If the thread begins to fray while working, do not continue. Finish the thread off neatly and begin again.

To begin, cut a length of stranded yarn approximately 12in (30cm) and divide this into separate strands. Smooth each strand between finger and thumb before regrouping and threading the needle. Do not tie a knot in the end, as this will make the finished work lumpy. Pull the needle through from the front of the fabric, leaving a tail of about 2in (5cm) on the right side. Hold this tail securely while the first stitch is worked. When several stitches are completed, the tail can be threaded onto a needle and taken through to the back of the work and then woven through the back of worked stitches.

The working thread can become tangled and twisted through the needle actions. Let the needle drop and hang freely – the thread will untwist itself.

Blocks of colour

To embroider a block of cross stitches in one colour, first work a row of half cross stitches, either horizontally or vertically. When the row is completed, work in the reverse direction completing the cross. Always work the top stitch of each cross stitch in the same direction on any piece of embroidery.

Scattered stitches
If stitches of one colour are scattered in small groups on the chart, do not fasten the thread off after each block, but take the thread through to the reverse of the fabric and secure with the needle away from the area being worked. Using another needle, continue to follow the chart until the first colour is required again. This method should only be used when working in a small area, otherwise the fabric may become puckered.

Large areas
When covering a large area it is advisable to work in horizontal rows. The first diagonal of each stitch should be completed from right to left. Then by working back along this row from left to right, the cross stitches will be formed. Continue to build up each colour block by working each successive row in the same way.

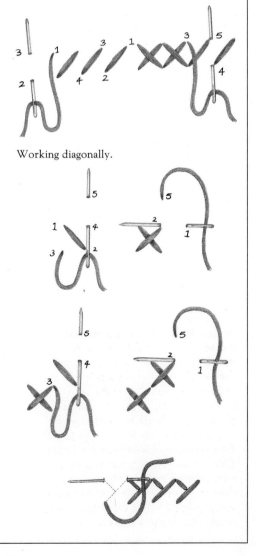

Working cross stitch
Cross stitch can be worked in rows from right to left or left to right, over any number of threads.
1 Bring the needle through at 1, insert diagonally at 2, bring out again at 3. Insert again at 4 to make the next slanting stitch.
2 To complete the cross, work back in the opposite direction. From 3, go diagonally down to 4 and out at 5.

Working diagonally.

Working diagonally
1 Bring the needle through at 1, go diagonally down to 2, across to 3, insert at 4, come out at 5.
2 From 5, go diagonally down to 1 and out at 2.
3 Go diagonally up to 4 and out at 5.

Half cross stitches
Sometimes, single diagonal stitches can be used on the edge of a design to achieve a rounded edge. Where this is required, diagonal lines, usually in the thread colour required, are printed across the pattern square.

Three-quarter and quarter stitch
The three-quarter stitch is made with the first half of a cross, then by stitching from the other top or bottom corner to the centre. The quarter stitch is worked from the corner of the cross to the centre of the square.

Working diagonally
To work diagonal lines of cross stitches, work downwards or upwards as shown opposite and complete each cross before beginning the next stitch.

Filling shapes
When filling a shape with colour, begin by embroidering across its widest point. Try to bring the needle up through unworked fabric and down through holes where stitches have already been worked.

FOLLOWING A CHART
The cross stitch designs in this book are all worked from graphed charts in which each coloured square represents one cross stitch. A colour key is given with each chart for identifying the embroidery thread numbers.

The centre of the chart is indicated by the arrows on each side. This coincides with the basting stitches worked to mark the middle of the fabric. The instructions given with each project tell you to begin working the embroidery from the middle of the design.

FINISHING
Remove the embroidery from its frame. Snip and pull out any basting stitches. Snip off any stray threads from the back of the work wherever possible, but be careful not to cut too close to your stitching. Remove masking tape from the fabric edges if it has been used.

Press the work lightly on the wrong side using a steam iron to smooth the fabric and 'emboss' the stitches.

If you are storing the finished

EMBROIDERY STITCHES
There are literally hundreds of embroidery stitches to choose from when you are decorating fabric. Here are some that are used in this book.

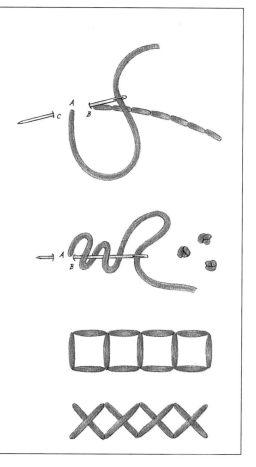

Back stitch
This stitch is used often in this book, usually to define a design line. It can be worked in straight lines or in curves. Bring the needle through at A, insert it at B and bring it out at C in front of A.

French knot
French knots are used single or massed in groups. Bring the needle through at A, wind the thread round the needle twice and then insert the point at B, close by A. Pull the thread through so that the knot tightens on the fabric surface.

Four-sided square stitch
This is ideal for stitching along an edge of a piece of fabric that you then want to fray. On the front the stitch looks like a square box while on the back it is a cross stitch.

embroidery, do not fold it. Store it flat in white, acid-free tissue paper.

FRAMING EMBROIDERY PICTURES

Consideration should be given to whether to frame the embroidery yourself or to take it to a professional. It should, however, be delivered for framing already mounted on backing card. The type of frame should be carefully chosen and any framer familiar with framing textiles should be able to advise on this. Very fine work should be mounted behind glass to protect it from dust and atmospheric polution, but raised embroidery will be flattened and should be left unglazed. The most important consideration is that the glass should not touch the embroidery. A special spray can be used to give some protection to work framed without glass. Unglazed pictures can be given a slightly padded look by inserting a layer of wadding between the embroidery and the cardboard mount.

It is possible to purchase non-reflective glass for framing, but this tends to alter the colours in the work very slightly, as it has a grey tinge.

MOUNTING EMBROIDERY ON BACKING CARD

To prepare embroidery for framing cut a sheet of white mounting card to the size of the frame rebate. Trim the embroidery fabric back to 2in (5cm) larger than the mounting card all round. Centre the embroidery on the card, right side up. Fold the top and bottom edges of the embroidery to the back of the card, then fold the side edges over. Push pins into the edges of the card all round to hold the fabric in place. Gently pull the fabric taut as you pin, so that the embroidery lies smooth and taut.

Using a strong needle and a long length of thread doubled and knotted, lace from side to side across the back of the work, starting in the middle of one side and pulling the fabric firmly with each stitch. Work the long sides first and then the

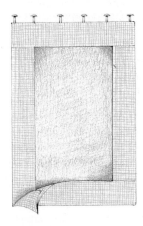

Fold the edges to the back and pin.

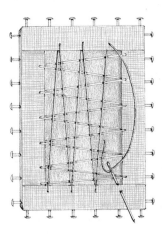

Lace from side to side then top to bottom.

short, keeping the embroidery centred on the card. Continue until the embroidery is completely stretched and securely held. Secure the fabric edges to the card with strips of masking tape.

Oval or round frames

When mounting an embroidery in an oval or a round frame, do not remove the centre-marking basting stitches. Using a soft pencil, mark the mounting card (usually supplied with the frame) horizontally and vertically through the centre point. Lay the embroidery face down on a clean surface and match up the marks on the card with the basting stitches. When the mount is accurately placed, lightly pencil around it on the fabric. Now remove the basting threads and cut out the embroidery along the pencilled line. Back the embroidery with lightweight iron-on fusible interfacing and then fuse to the cardboard mount. The embroidery is then ready to frame.

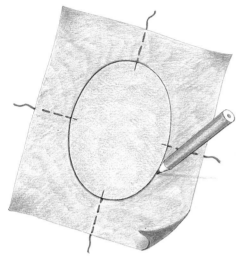

Line up the basting threads and pencil around.

An alternative method is to use the oval or round cardboard mount as a template, tracing the shape on to the wrong side of the embroidery. Trim the excess fabric away, leaving a 2in (5cm) turning allowance from the pencil line.

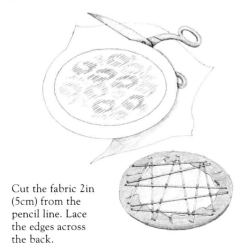

Cut the fabric 2in (5cm) from the pencil line. Lace the edges across the back.

Run a gathering thread ½in (1cm) inside the pencilled line. Put the cardboard mount in position and draw up the fabric evenly, adjusting the gathers. Finish with a double back stitch to secure the gathers. To finish, either lace across the back of the work with strong thread or secure the fabric edges to the card mount with masking tape.

Self-adhesive mounting card
Special mounting card can be bought that consists of a piece of card with a self-adhesive front. This enables the embroidery to be mounted securely and permanently without fraying. Then the mount and embroidery together can be cut to the exact shape required using a scalpel and rule.

GREETINGS CARDS
Small cross stitch motifs are ideal for personalized greetings cards. A small design can usually be worked in just a few hours and provides a distinctive message that will be treasured by the recipient. Ready-made greetings-card blanks with cut-out windows can be purchased in a wide range of sizes and styles.

Cards can also be made at home, using thin card or construction paper. Draw out the shape of the envelope, but about ⅛in (3mm) smaller all round. Draw the same shape to the right and left of the first one. Then draw and cut a window in the middle section. Score and fold along the division lines.

Mounting the embroidery
When the embroidery is finished, press it lightly on the wrong side with a warm iron. Trim the fabric so that the motif is displayed centrally in the window. Spread clear, all-purpose glue thinly around the edges of the window on the inside of the card. Press the embroidery down on to the glued card, checking to see that its position is correct before finally pressing down. Fold and stick the left-hand panel down over the back of the embroidery. Leave to dry.

Acknowledgements
The author would like to thank the
following suppliers for their help with
the book:

Coats Patons Crafts
PO Box McMullen Road
Darlington
Co Durham DL1 1YQ
for stranded cottons, small picture
frames, coloured picture mounts and
card mounts.

MacGregor Designs
PO Box 129
Burton-on-Trent
DE14 3XH
for the wooden pincushion.

Framecraft Miniatures
372–376 Summer Lane
Hockley
Birmingham B19 3QA
for the clock, bell-pull hangers, candle
screen and Christmas tree frame.

Stranded cotton substitution chart					
Anchor	**DMC**	**Anchor**	**DMC**	**Anchor**	**DMC**
1	blanc	265	989	371	433
23	819	266	3347	376	842
29	891	267	3346	379	840
38	355	288	445	388	3782
46	666	289	307	393	640
47	304	290	973	403	310
50	605	291	444	410	995
55	604	293	727	885	3047
59	326	295	726	1002	977
92	162	298	972	1006	304
98	553	300	3078	1007	3772
131	798	301	745	1009	3770
133	796	302	743	1010	951
142	820	304	741	1020	3713
146	798	311	676	1023	3712
209	562	323	722	1024	3328
215	320	328	3341	1025	347
225	954	329	947	1030	3746
229	700	335	606	1036	3750
230	909	340	919	1038	519
239	702	347	402	1039	518
242	913	352	300	1041	535
243	912	359	801	1044	895
244	911	363	436	1047	402
254	907	367	739	5975	356
258	904	370	434	9575	758